POCKET WISDOM SERIES

Renewal

A LITTLE BOOK OF

COURAGE & HOPE

BY EKNATH EASWARAN

NILGIRI PRESS

The selections in this book are taken from

Eknath Easwaran's Your Life Is Your Message.

ISBN: 978-1-58638-034-2

Library of Congress Control Number: 2008942445

Printed on 100% postconsumer recycled paper

Publisher's Cataloging-in-Publication block

will be found on the last leaf of this book.

A reading of this book is available as a download

from our Web site: www.easwaran.org

The Blue Mountain Center of Meditation publishes

books on how to lead a spiritual life in the home and

community. The Center also teaches Eknath Easwaran's

program of passage meditation at retreats.

TABLE OF CONTENTS

INTRODUCTION

PART ONE: RENEWAL BEGINS WITH ME

PART TWO: RENEWING RELATIONSHIPS

PART THREE: THE UNITY OF LIFE

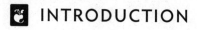 INTRODUCTION

◆ A MESSAGE OF RENEWAL

CONSERVATION BIOLOGISTS CALL THE elephant a "keystone" species. Just as an arch cannot stand without its keystone, many other species, and sometimes entire ecosystems, would be lost without the elephant. On the African savannah, the elephant's foraging creates a mixture of woodlands and grasslands, making the savannah hospitable to many more creatures, from the zebra to the giraffe to the baboon. In drier climates, it provides water not only for itself but for all the other species by creating new water holes and even digging wells. Because of the elephant, a huge, hungry animal with gentle habits, the entire ecosystem flourishes.

Today, because of our skills and technology, human society has assumed the position of keystone in the vast, delicately balanced arch of nature. Like the elephants in the forest, our lives affect all the other creatures, plants, and elements around us. They all depend on us for support and protection.

As we now know only too well, our influence is often far from benign. Rather than supporting the rest of life, human beings seem to be at odds with it. Scientists tell us that many of our social and business activities are not only driving other species to extinction but are threatening the water, soil, climate, and atmosphere on which our lives depend. We seem to have trouble even relating to our own species. International crises, the tension and alienation of our inner cities, the increase in poverty and homelessness, the drug abuse and high suicide rate among our young people all suggest that we lack the wisdom to protect our-selves, let alone the rest of nature.

Yet in another sense, today there is great prom-ise of renewal. Around the world – even in some of the countries most troubled by poverty or civil war or pollution – many thoughtful people are making a deep, concerted search for a new way of life. Their efforts, which rarely reach headlines, are among the most important events occurring today. Sometimes these people call themselves peace workers, at other times environmentalists, but most of the time they work in humble ano-nymity. They are simply quiet people changing the world by changing themselves.

The purpose of this book is to encourage those people and the changes they are making. In it, I hope to underscore the tremendous potential of such "tremendous trifles," to use G.K. Chesterton's phrase, for improving our lives and the world we live in, and I will be offering some practical suggestions on how to make those changes more satisfying and powerful.

Through such unobtrusive, almost invisible

work, the changes we would like to see in the world around us can begin immediately in our own lives, making us more secure, more contented, and more effective. Each of us has the capacity to become a healing and protecting force in the family, with friends, at work, in the community, in the environment.

A SIMPLE, LOVING LIFE

SUCH LITTLE CHANGES CAN SEEM painfully small when compared to the kinds of crises we read about in the headlines, but through my personal experience I have become convinced that there is no instrument of change more powerful than the well-lived life. Having had the privilege of growing up in Gandhi's India, walking with him, studying his life, and trying to live by his example, I can say that his simple, loving life has done more to benefit the world than all the speeches and policies composed by politicians – however eloquent, however well-meaning.

Once, while Mahatma Gandhi's train was pulling slowly out of the station, a reporter ran up to him and asked for a message to take back to his people. Gandhi's reply was a hurried line scrawled on a scrap of paper: "My life is my message."

The great spiritual teachers of all religions – men and women like Francis of Assisi, Teresa of Avila, the Compassionate Buddha, Mahatma Gandhi – all say, "You start with yourself." There is not much purpose served by preaching to others or by talking at them. The only way to influence people for the better – your family, your friends, your club, your class, your clinic, your society, even your enemies – is through your personal example.

When you are able to live with joy, giving your time and energy to improving the quality of life for all, you are not only fulfilling your highest destiny, you are also helping all those around you to grow to their fullest height. As you will see from the challenges outlined in this book, this is not an easy path. Self-transformation is arduous work, especially at first; but each tiny change brings with it the joyful awareness that your life is gradually becoming a force for peaceful change.

This call for renewal challenges each of us to undertake the search for a sustainable, fully satisfying way of life, based not on exploiting the external environment but by taking advantage of the riches within us – the nobility, compassion, and desire for peace that lie hidden in every heart. This is not work that can be done for us by corporations or governments; we have to do it ourselves.

☕ WORKING TOGETHER

YET WE DO NOT HAVE TO DO IT ALONE. My grandmother, who was my spiritual teacher, always used the tamarind tree to illustrate the power of ordinary people. The tamarind is a big tree, with very small, thin leaves. On a hot day, the people of my old state of Kerala like to sleep in its shade. The leaves are so numerous and are packed so closely together that they protect us from the tropical sun just as if they were one large canopy. "Little Lamp, you don't have to look for big people," Granny would tell me. "Look for little people like yourself, then band together and work in harmony."

So don't be intimidated by position or power or wealth. If little people like you and me work together, we can do a great deal to transform the world. Taken together, these small daily efforts to improve our ordinary lives live up to a very powerful force that, in the years to come, can become a kind of spiritual revolution, providing a firm foundation for the kind of political, economic, and ecological improvements we need to make.

PART ONE

Renewal Begins with Me

🐛 SHEDDING AN OLD SKIN

DURING THE MONSOON TIME IN KERALA, the state in South India from which I come, the paddy fields stretch like an endless emerald carpet towards the horizon. It is a time of great growth and joy for all creatures. As a little boy, I used to walk beside my grandmother across those rice fields to our ancestral temple.

As we walked, I would often see the cast-off skin of a snake, lying like a lace ribbon beside the path. One day, I asked Granny, "Why do these snakes have to lose their skin?" Her reply was full of wisdom. I realize now that she was speaking of more than snakes.

"If snakes do not shed their skin," she replied, "they cannot grow. They will suffocate in their old skin." I often remember her words. Today we too need to grow. The intense restlessness of our young people, the dissatisfaction and stifled idealism which haunts so many older people – these are signs that our society is ready to shed an outworn definition of who we are and what we can become.

While I appreciate the attempts made by governments and distinguished groups and some corporations to solve our environmental or social problems, the solution lies ultimately in your hands and mine. What kind of image do we have of ourselves? What is our purpose in living?

By undertaking to answer those questions from our own experience, we will be laying the foundations of a truly sustainable society.

🐾 WAKING UP

IT IS SAID THAT WHEN THE COM-
passionate Buddha entered a town, he radi-
ated such security and joy that crowds gathered
around him just to gaze at his face. "Blessed One,"
they asked timidly, "are you a god?"

"No," he said.

"Are you an angel?"

"No."

"Are you a prophet?"

"No."

"Then what are you?"

"I am awake."

This is the literal, etymological meaning of the
word *Buddha*, from the Sanskrit root *budh*, "to
wake up."

When I was teaching at a university in India, I
believed I was fully conscious, fully awake. I was

quite certain that all my colleagues were awake and that even my students were awake. I was fully active in what we normally call waking life: pursuing private satisfactions, making money, accumulating material possessions, trying to get recognition. Such a life, the Buddha would say with compassion, is the life of a somnambulist. I was sleep-walking, sleep-teaching, sleep-living.

Today, if we look around, we can see that we live in a sleeping society – asleep and dreaming of wealth and pleasure and power even as the environmental foundations of our lives are being eroded by the unconscious forces of greed, ignorance, and hostility.

It is only when you wake up that you begin to see that there is a whole other world inside of you, as real as the world without. In that inner world lies the key to healing the world around us.

🐦 A CONTINUING SOURCE OF JOY

I believe that if one man gains spiritually
the whole world gains with him and,
if one man falls, the whole world falls
to that extent. – MAHATMA GANDHI

WE ARE ALL INCLINED TO GET OVER-whelmed at times and to ask, "What can I, one person, do to right problems like pollution and hunger?" Gandhi's reply is simple but challenging: you just raise your own consciousness and you will raise the consciousness of the entire world. That is what he did.

All of us can give a great gift to the world by looking at our life and gradually removing from it the things that are not simple and beautiful. I am terribly saddened to see in the papers how many people, both old and young, are sleeping through cold winter nights under the bridges and on the pavement in San Francisco. Can you imagine? Even in the richest country on the face of the earth, many people have no place to sleep.

I regard these people as my kith and kin, just as I regard the hungry children of Africa as my own. That is what happens when you begin to be aware that the Self, the Lord of Love dwelling in your heart, is the same as the Self in all these desperate people. When you see this unity, you will find a continuing source of joy in making wise use of your money, your time, your energy, your resources in the service of all.

NATURE WITH A CAPITAL N

WHEN MY WIFE AND I WERE LIVING WITH my mother on the Blue Mountain in India, we came to know a European couple who lived nearby. They were always very hospitable to us, but the husband had an aversion to the word "God." Whenever I said "God," he would correct me: "Nature with a capital N." This did not bother me at all, since in India's five-thousand-year-old tradition there are many authorities who state that God has countless different names, while there are just as many who say that the ultimate reality is not He or She but It, and has no name at all. So when my friend would greet me and ask me how my mother was, I would answer, "Very well, thank you, thanks to the grace of Nature with a capital N."

When I was first in Berkeley, I discovered that America has its share of individualists as well. There were occasions at Christmastime when I would say, "Hey, Tom, have a Merry Christmas," and Tom would say, "I don't believe in Christianity." Then I would say, "Happy Hanukkah!" and he would say, "I don't believe in Judaism either." So I would just say, "Have a nice day!"

None of these things makes any difference. When I talk about the Self, or what the traditional religions call God, I am not talking about somebody outside of you, swinging in a heavenly hammock between the Milky Way and Andromeda galaxies. I am talking about someone who is inside of you all the time – the resident of your deepest consciousness, who is waiting to be discovered, calling out to be courted. As Meister Eckhart says, "God is in, we are out; God is at home, we are abroad."

PATIENCE

PATIENCE IS ONE OF THE MOST VALUABLE allies in the difficult journey of self-transformation. As St. Francis says, "It is in pardoning that we are pardoned." When you are able to be patient with others, you can be patient with yourself, and that will give you all the inner support you need to persevere and make the changes you want to make in your life. But patience can't be acquired overnight. It's just like building up a muscle. Every day you need to work on it, to push its limits. When people tell me they don't have any patience, I always say, "That's only because you've never pushed it."

Every day I push my patience. Whenever people provoke me or cause me difficulties (which is seldom, but it does happen), I don't get agitated or give up on them or try to be critical. I say to myself, "Here's a chance to extend my patience. Let me bear with him until he falls down, and then help him get up. Let me bear with her until she comes around, and then work with her in a worthy cause." That kind of gritting your teeth and bearing it, establishing your roots deeper and deeper in your consciousness, can bring you, as Gandhi proved, an endurance that no government or corporation or institution can shake.

In India, God is called "the ocean of patience." Look at all that we are doing to the earth, yet because God is an ocean of patience, when we learn to be patient with ourselves and others, we become humble instruments in his hands.

THE SECOND HALF OF LIFE

I am the feminine qualities: fame, beauty,
perfect speech, memory, intelligence, loyalty,
and forgiveness. — BHAGAVAD GITA

PEOPLE WHO IDENTIFY THEMSELVES WITH their body often find the latter half of life a great burden. Only when you learn to identify yourself with the Self will the latter half of your life become a great blessing.

Once, when a friend and I were walking at the local shopping district, a young woman reporter stopped me. She apologized for interrupting my walk and said, "Do you mind if I ask you a question?" She cleared her throat. "What would you say is the most unpleasant thing about growing old?"

I wasn't offended. She was just reflecting the

assumptions which underlie all our modern attitudes. So I smiled and said, "The latter part of my life is wonderful. In fact, there is no comparison with the first part. All the physical vigor and all the running about and the . . . what do you call it? – the vim and razzle-dazzle of early life, it's all 'sound and fury, signifying nothing.'"

When you have only your physical appearance to depend on, I might have added if I had known her better, there is no escape from the ravages of time. That is why spiritual teachers say, "Enjoy your youth, but don't neglect to light the lamp of beauty inside, which will glow brighter with the passage of time."

Our society lives by the theory that beauty and joy are limited to a particular period in life. It's true that children have a marvelous beauty of their own, but every child has to grow up. Teenagers have a certain beauty of their own, but they, too, have to grow up. Similarly, the twenty-somethings and the thirty-somethings will eventually become forty- and fifty-somethings.

When my grandmother, in her sixties, came and sat with us in our ancestral home, she was the center of attention. Her beauty came entirely from within, a beauty born of the highest feminine qualities. Forgiveness, inward strength, the use of gentle words (which means gentle thoughts), all play a part in making a woman – or a man! – beautiful.

Whatever religion you belong to, whatever country you belong to, everybody responds to this kind of inner beauty. You don't have to advertise. To use one of the great similes from Sri Ramakrishna, you will be like a lotus opening in the rays of the morning sun. The lotus doesn't need to say, "Where are the bees?" The bees are looking for the lotus. All of us, inwardly, are looking for this kind of beauty and love that grows with the passage of time.

❦ HARNESSING ANGER

JUST AS WE LIVE IN AN EXTERNAL, physical world, we live at the same time in an internal world of thoughts, feelings, and desires. While our modern civilization has made great strides in understanding the external world and using it for our comfort, we have barely begun to explore the inner world. Only now are we beginning to recognize that the forces in this internal world – forces like anger, greed, and fear – have the power to devastate the mind, despoil the earth, and destroy human beings. We need to learn how these winds blow, how they can be directed, and how they can be put to work.

In the countryside where I live, I often see windmills harnessing the power of the wind, pumping water from deep beneath the earth to feed the local dairy cows and irrigate crops.

Windmills put the wind to work. Similarly, you can set up an anger mill, which will put your anger to work, drawing the living waters of compassion and creativity from the depths of your heart to help all those around you.

Gandhi learned this secret in South Africa. "I have learnt through bitter experience," he wrote, "the one supreme lesson to conserve my anger, and as heat conserved is transmuted into energy, even so our anger controlled can be transmuted into a power which can move the world." Gandhiji is not quoting a book or telling us what his teacher said. He is speaking from his own experience.

Harnessing his anger about the indignities that were heaped upon him and others in South Africa, he changed the world.

🍎 LIVING TO BE ONE HUNDRED AND TWENTY

IT IS VITAL TO UNDERSTAND THE LAWS of mental dynamics. These inner forces and their effects on our external world have been studied in detail by many of the world's great spiritual figures, who have cast off the spell of separateness and awakened to the unity of all life; the ancient sages of India have especially studied how the mind can influence the body.

One of the sages' surprisingly prescient theories starts with the hypothesis that there is a fixed number of times the heart is meant to beat each year; the number they gave was forty million. While there may be some argument about the precise number, I think it is not too hard to agree that the heart, like any sturdy pump, has a limited working span.

Now here is the brilliant touch, which is close to certain areas of modern heart research. Positive emotions, the sages say, are always slower and less stressful than negative ones. You can observe it in yourself. The next time you are getting angrier and angrier and are about to "blow your top," check your pulse and breathing rhythm. They have all speeded up. The entire physiological system has been thrown into overdrive.

In modern heart research, doctors speak of people with "high-risk factors" like a tendency toward anger or competitiveness, leading to high blood pressure and an increased risk of heart disease. The sages of ancient India used a different vocabulary, but the message is similar: when we are frequently angry or afraid or agitated, they say, our forty million beats last only about ten months, instead of twelve. We have lost two months of our life.

On the bright side, the sages give some practical advice which accords with recent suggestions by respected researchers in the fields of heart disease and psychoneuroimmunology: if you can be patient under attack, not retaliating but not retreating either, if you can learn to return good will for ill will and even help those who are unkind to you, then your forty million beats, instead of lasting for twelve months, will last for fourteen. You have gained two months of life. By the sages' calculations, living for the benefit of others should enable us to live to a full span of one hundred and twenty years of active, loving service to the world.

PARKING THE MIND
IN KINDNESS

A GREAT BONUS THAT COMES WHEN THE mind slows down over a long period is that you become a stranger to insecurity and depression. When the mind is going fast, depression is always with you, riding along in the back seat. When the mind is going slow, enabling you to choose freely which thoughts you think, depression is outside, hitchhiking. You just say, "Sorry, no room," and drive right by.

I am not talking about morality but dynamics. When your car is going fast, you cannot turn or stop. That is a perfect image of the speeded-up mind as it heads for a crash – whether it is rushing in anger, or fear, or greed.

If you want to park your car in the city, you have to get off the freeway, slow down gradually from sixty miles per hour to forty to twenty to a complete halt, then carefully shift into reverse and perform that amazing feat called parallel parking. Similarly, in order to live in inner freedom, you have to learn how to slow down your mind, bring it to a restorative stillness, and park it anywhere you like – in patience, say, or compassion, or love.

It's an amazing skill. I have a few friends who are very skilled at parking in San Francisco. In places where I see almost no room between two cars, they are able to gracefully slip the car in – even on some of San Francisco's steepest streets. When you can do this with your mind, you will find that nothing can upset you. No matter what happens, you can keep your mind securely parked in kindness and understanding. Even one person who has mastered this skill can begin to transform the community where he or she lives.

TRANSFORMING GREED

WHENEVER THE WORLD'S PROBLEMS SEEM overwhelming, remember that you have a vast reservoir of energy and creativity within you, which can provide all the resources you need to make a lasting contribution.

All the negative forces in the mind, if you can only win them over to your side, can become your friends.

That is how Gandhi brought about such monumental changes. It was not only anger that he learned to harness. According to his friend Sardar Patel, Gandhi found a tremendous source of beneficial power in greed as well.

Patel tells a delightful story about a train journey with Gandhi. At every stop, Gandhi would get off and circulate among the crowd with his begging bowl, collecting for the poorest of India's poor. Jewelry, watches, money – he collected any-thing. And he collected from everyone – men, women, children, rich, poor. Even the beggars were not exempt from his appeals. As Patel, who couldn't resist pulling Gandhi's leg now and then, and a companion watched this strange, wonderful scene, Patel said if you want to see a human being consumed by greed, look no further.

That is what I call the magic of transformation. Instead of just being greedy for himself, Gandhi had become greedy for all. He handled millions of rupees without a trace of personal greed. Everything was for his work, nothing for himself.

PROUD HUMILITY

*There comes a time when an individual
becomes irresistible and his action becomes
all-pervasive in its effect. This comes when
he reduces himself to zero.*

— MAHATMA GANDHI

"PERSONALLY," ST. FRANCIS OF ASSISI
would say, "I'm nobody. But," he'll add, "do you
know who has come to life in my life? Do you
know who lives in my heart?"

Gandhi had the same mixture of pride, ambition, and utter meekness. When he was asked,
"Don't you want to be president of India?" he said,
"No. I want to make myself zero. But I want my
actions to benefit all of mankind."

In my own life, when I was starting out on this
path, many of my relatives and friends told me,

"You have such capacities, such promise – why do you want to throw it all away? Don't you have any ambition?" If they were to ask me that question today, I would say that I simply was not ambitious before. That is why I was content with being a writer and a teacher of literature. Now, in this country of very ambitious people, I have become one of the most ambitious of all.

So as you begin to simplify your life, if people ask you why you don't have any ambition, please tell them that you are only now learning what ambition is.

🍏 BE A WORK OF ART

GREAT SCRIPTURES LIKE THE BHAGAVAD Gita can be looked upon as artist's manuals. Just as painters study their color and drawing manuals, you can read the Gita or the Sermon on the Mount as a living manual to help you make your life a flawless work of art.

This is truly the supreme art. When your life becomes a work of art, your family will benefit from it every day.

When I entered Gandhi's ashram in central India, close to my university, there was not a single artistic artifact there – not even carved driftwood. In those days I was very culturally oriented, looking for beauty in all kinds of external objects, but when the cottage door opened, at five in the evening, and a brown, blessed figure came out, I saw the greatest statue I have ever seen in my life. The greatest painting I have ever seen came to life. That's the highest ideal for a human being.

PART TWO

Renewing Relationships

HAPPINESS

ONCE I ASKED MY TEACHER, MY GRAND-mother, why a certain man in our village never seemed to be happy, even though he had all of life's advantages – he was healthy, he had a fine family and a good job, and he even had a full head of hair. Her reply was simple but profound: "It is not possible for life to make a selfish person happy, whatever temporary satisfactions may come along. But," she added, "life cannot but give you joy if you live for the joy of others."

LIVING AT LIFE'S CENTER

ONLY A FEW CENTURIES AGO BRIGHT people all over Europe believed that the sun and stars and planets orbited around the earth. Some of the greatest geniuses in the West – Archimedes, Plato, Aristotle, Dante – were absolutely certain that the earth was the center of the universe. It took one man, Copernicus, to knock the bottom out of this theory.

Today we all learn in kindergarten that the sun, not the earth, is the center of the solar system, and that even the sun is but one among billions in a galaxy that is one among billions. But if we look into the world within, which is as real as the world without, we shall find to our consternation that each of us still believes that we are the center of the world. When we say "I love you," what we usually mean is, "I'll do anything for you, provided you accept that I am the center of the universe and keep a steady orbit around me and my desires."

As a professor and as a teacher of meditation, I have lived around young people for over fifty years, and I have had many opportunities to hear Juliet say to Romeo, "Everything will be wonderful if you just keep going around me, because I am the center of the universe." And Romeo replies, "Sure, honey, as long as you keep going around me, since I am the center of the universe." Most of the problems we have in the world today arise because we or our company or our nation live on the circumference of life, trying to make the rest of the world orbit around us.

As you learn gradually to understand the real needs of those around you, you will be not unlike Copernicus discovering for our benefit that the earth is not at the center of the solar system. You will be discovering that the individual ego can never be the center of the universe. It is the Self, dwelling in the hearts of all, who is at the center.

You will begin to understand some of the words that are used by great mystics to describe God.

Plotinus, for example, calls God "the One." He doesn't say "Supreme Reality," or the "Clear Light," but simply, "the One": "So we always move round the One – if we did not, we should dissolve and cease to exist – but we do not always look towards the One." It is God who is at the center, and this center is in the very depths of our consciousness.

❦ EXPAND YOUR CAPACITY TO LOVE

ONE OF THE REASONS WE HAVE SO MANY interpersonal problems today is that everyone is constantly being encouraged to concentrate entirely on himself or herself. When you dwell on yourself like this, preoccupied with private profit and personal pleasure, you lose your resilience. A little knock at the door explodes like a pistol shot; a little cracking of knuckles sounds like a machine gun.

On the other hand, when you gradually expand your capacity to love, beginning with your family, but eventually extending to your country, and even the whole world, including the birds of the air and beasts of the field, you will become very secure. If somebody says or does anything against you, you will feel badly for them. It is not that you will be unaware or that you will connive with them. You will be so secure inwardly that your love will not be affected by anything they say or do. Instead of retaliating, you will be able to give the "soft answer that turneth away wrath."

Such an attitude is beautifully infectious. People – especially children – learn to love through osmosis. Don't think children are as unsophisticated as they are made out to be. When little Johnny is looking at you with those quizzical eyes, or little

Emily is snapping her gum, they are seeing right through you. And they are absorbing what they see.

I once heard a story about a mynah bird which developed a very distressing cough. His owner took him to the vet, who listened to the mynah's cough and then said to the owner, "Let me hear you cough." It was the same cough. So the doctor said, "You get over your cough, and the mynah bird will get over your cough too." Similarly, if we want our children to grow up secure and loving, we should turn our backs on profit and pleasure and devote ourselves to putting those around us first.

That is how a home becomes beautiful. I appreciate beauty but, when I visit a home, I am not impressed with expensive furniture and exotic art and elegant gardens. That's not where beauty comes from. It is when I see a family living together with deep affection, each person putting the other's needs first, that I say to myself, "What a beautiful home!" This is my idea of the beautiful home – where the father, the mother, and the children always remember the unity of the home, where they turn their backs on their own personal pursuits, on their own personal pleasure and profit, to work together for a higher goal. It is not easy, but it will enable the parents, the children, and even the pets, to flourish.

🪷 FAMILY YOGA

They live in wisdom who see themselves in all and all in them. —BHAGAVAD GITA

IT IS GOOD TO EXTEND YOUR LOVING relationships to include more and more people. I live with a large extended family of friends, which includes people of many ages, races, and backgrounds, and I relate to everybody very closely. One of the great joys in this way of life is the opportunity to watch your family grow to include your neighbors, your whole community, and eventually the world.

Once Mahatma Gandhi's wife was asked how many children she had, and she said, "I have only four but my husband has four hundred million." What that means for us is that nobody is childless. All the world's children are our children.

Anybody who does anything to harm the future of the earth is doing harm to their own children.

Our ultimate goal is the realization that while there are billions of people in the world, there is only one Self. This realization opens a perennial fountain of love in your heart. You see yourself in all and everybody in yourself. When any child is hungry, whether in Africa or Asia or in our own country, your love will release a flood of energy and creativity to help alleviate that hunger.

🐾 DHARMAPUTRA AND HIS DOG

THERE IS A STORY FROM THE INDIAN tradition that beautifully illustrates the compassion for all creatures which is the keynote of spiritual ecology. There once lived a king called

Dharmaputra, who was the soul of virtue and compassion. When the time came for him to shed his body, he ascended to heaven accompanied by a dog. When he reached heaven's gate, the Indian equivalent of St. Peter looked up his name. "Let's see . . . Dharmaputra. Yes, we have orders to let you in. But we don't have any listing for a dog."

"Won't you please look again?" asked Dharmaputra.

So St. Peter looked up all the rules and said, "I'm sorry, but there is no provision here for dogs."

Dharmaputra did not hesitate. "That dog loves me," he said. "Wherever I go, he goes too, so I have got to take him with me."

St. Peter again considered all the relevant records. "Rules are rules," he said finally. "Either you come in alone, or you go back."

Dharmaputra didn't budge. He said simply, "No dog, no me."

Then a miracle took place. Suddenly, instead of a dog, it was Sri Krishna, the Lord of Love, standing at Dharmaputra's side. St. Peter opened the gates, and, in my version of the story, as Dharmaputra entered heaven Sri Krishna leaned over and whispered, "That was a close shave, wasn't it?"

Little stories like this can remind us to always be compassionate towards our fellow creatures, recognizing that the same Self lives in them as in us.

For a spiritual ecologist, every creature is sacred. We can do a great deal for the earth by introducing our children to stories like these, and by helping them to cultivate loving relationships with animals and birds. It's very good for them, and it's very good for the creatures too.

🐾 A LITTLE GESTURE

SELF-WILL, THE ENEMY OF UNITY, OFTEN expresses itself in small but powerful likes and dislikes, which disrupt our relationships even if we and the people around us are not entirely aware of it. When we learn to reduce our self-will, and become a little more aware of the needs of others, we can renew our relationships in subtle and not-so-subtle ways.

I had a clear example of this when I was teaching at my university in India. Throughout my teaching career I have been very fond of the blackboard, getting to the classroom early and filling the board with assignments and recondite Sanskrit and English vocabulary. Unfortunately, the English department used rather small black-boards, so I had my eye on the physics depart-ment, which had the biggest blackboards on campus. I contacted the physics faculty, and one of them kindly allowed me to use his lecture hall.

The blackboard was spacious, and I was quite comfortable, except for one thing. Beneath the blackboard was a running groove for the chalk. Every day when I arrived, I found the chalk resting at the far left end of this groove. Since I am right-handed, I moved the chalk to the right end and left it there when I finished.

I didn't think much about it. Every day when I arrived I would say to myself, "Why should this chap always leave the chalk on the left-hand side?" and take it back to the right. Eventually even the students got into the act and enjoyed our confusion.

Then one day it struck me that my physics counterpart must be left-handed. For a few days I left the chalk at the left corner. To my surprise,

I began to find the chalk placed carefully at the right corner for me.

Sometimes it takes only a little gesture, a little extra awareness, to renew our relationships.

A SHIELD AGAINST DEJECTION

> *Love your enemies, bless them that*
> *curse you, do good to them that hate you, and*
> *pray for them which despitefully use you, and*
> *persecute you; that ye may be the children of*
> *your Father which is in heaven.*
>
> —THE SERMON ON THE MOUNT

AS FAR AS I KNOW, THERE IS NO GREATER thrill than that of winning over an enemy to be your friend. That's why Jesus, when he gives us those challenges in the Sermon on the Mount, says "Bless them that curse you." Such words are not meant to be declaimed in a pious tone from the pulpit but to be lived out in the storms and tempests, large and small, which life brings to all of us.

When someone hurts your feelings, or treads heavily on your pet opinion, that's the test. Jesus would say, "Let's see your daring! Do good to those that harm you – let us see your courage!"

I always suggest that you cultivate as many relationships as possible, working together with others who share our ideals. Then you will have plenty of opportunity to do things for each other rather than for yourself alone.

That's the kind of opportunity I had as I was growing up, and therein lies the genius of my teacher, my mother's mother, who fulfilled herself completely by always forgetting herself in the joy and the welfare of all those around. That is the only real cure for unhappiness.

It is a prescription that could come from any authentic spiritual physician. If you dwell upon yourself and your own private satisfactions, the first disappointment will throw you into despair. If you can train yourself to think more and more of the needs of all those around you, to work with people around you even if they are not always pleasant, you will be making yourself immune to dejection, and you will be helping others to do the same.

JUGGLING

I KNOW A LITTLE BIT ABOUT JUGGLING from my own personal experience. When I was in high school I was a bright student and I got tired of hearing my classmates say things like, "All he knows is books," or "Instead of blood he has ink in his veins," and other such things that passed for humor in my high school. I consulted my granny, and she said, "Why don't you learn to juggle?" So I took two lemons and started.

If you have ever tried to juggle, you will know that even with only two lemons it is much harder than it looks. Once the lemons are in motion, it seems like you're juggling not two but twenty-two. But I kept practicing and when I had mastered two, Granny said, "Why don't you add one more?" When I finally unveiled my new skill, my classmates were astonished.

Similarly, if you are really in love, you will find a great deal of joy in astonishing your partner, your family, or your friends with your ability to juggle effortlessly with your likes and dislikes.

For example, if you happen to take your partner

to a restaurant, you can give the menu to him or her and say, "You order what you like; that's what I will enjoy." You are so much in love that you can enjoy the other person's enjoyment. For the most part, this is pretty safe. Usually your partner will order responsibly for you. But once in a while you may end up with a dish that tastes like gall and wormwood. That will be your finals, the test of true love.

ONE THING AT A TIME

MANY YEARS AGO MY WIFE AND I TOOK a trip to Arizona. As we were driving along one of the beautiful roads there, I looked up to see a sign nailed to the top of a tree. It read, "You should be watching the road." I wanted to answer, "I'm not driving!" but I did appreciate the message.

There is almost a conspiracy in our modern media culture to fragment our attention. We are encouraged to talk on the phone while we drive, to watch television while we eat, to listen to the news while we jog. All these things deplete our capacity to concentrate and reduce our ability to love.

Children in particular suffer from this. When you are listening to a child, try to give your full attention. Those bright little eyes know when your attention is wandering. When the kids are giving you news from school, set your newspaper aside for a moment and listen to every word. You will be training them in how to love.

That's how I was trained by my grandmother. When I came back from school every day, Granny would say, "Tell me everything – from the time you left home until the time you came back." I knew that every part of my life was important to her.

So please try to give as much time as possible to your children. Giving them toys or money is not a substitute for this. They will grow up secure and generous, ready to make the world a better place.

☕ FILLING THE INNER NEEDS

VERY EARLY IN MY LIFE MY GRAND-mother helped me to develop a deep love of nature in a simple way. She did not rush me here and there for taking courses and acquiring skills; instead, she gave me lots of time to understand and admire the beauties of nature. She considered this the best use of my time and energy.

BUSINESS REPLY MAIL

FIRST-CLASS MAIL   PERMIT NO 1   TOMALES CA

THE BLUE MOUNTAIN CENTER OF MEDITATION

& NILGIRI PRESS

PO BOX 256

TOMALES CA 94971–9902

We hope you enjoy *Essence of the Upanishads.*

The Blue Mountain Center of Meditation, which Eknath Easwaran founded in 1961, publishes books offering timeless wisdom for daily living & gives retreats on Easwaran's method of passage meditation.

Please return this card if you would like to subscribe to

____ *Blue Mountain,* our free quarterly journal:

____ paper version by mail (within U.S. only)

____ email version

____ Free *Thought for the Day* by email

We look forward to hearing from you.

Name

Address

City / State / Zip

Email address (for *Blue Mountain* or *Thought for the Day*). We never share information or email lists.

Visit our
Web site

www.
easwaran.
org

Call us at
800 475 2369

I have great love for children, and I think we should be careful not to allow their childhood to be lost. While there is an important place for lessons and sports, it is not always doing them a valuable service to rush them from lesson to lesson.

In my understanding of human development, when our deep, basic needs – for loving attention, for plenty of time to think and understand and grow – are not met while we are still children, we often turn to less desirable means of satisfying them when we grow up.

I always try to give full credit to my grandmother and mother for any success that has come my way. They filled all my deepest needs by the time I left high school. Today, with no childhood needs that have to be met, I can enjoy life in full freedom. I have no special need for money or pleasure or profit or prestige: through the love of these two women I came to understand that these things won't add anything to me. When we are inwardly full, we have only one need: to give.

When children grow up with this kind of inner fullness, they have no need to exploit the environment. They can enjoy all the innocent joys of life while using their talents, time, and resources to protect the earth. According to an ancient Sanskrit saying, any parent who has raised such a child – a young man or woman who lives to give – has fulfilled their highest purpose in life.

NO LONGER RULED BY FEAR

THROUGH YEARS AND YEARS OF DIFFIcult practice, I have acquired a skill which more than repays the effort I spent. Now, on those occasions when somebody is discourteous to me, which is rare, I find it natural to be more courteous; when somebody is unkind, to be more kind; when somebody is moving away from me, to be more supportive.

This is how you renew your relationships. There is nobody who does not respond slowly, gradually, to this kind of love that tires out its opposition, a love that will not let you go. When we encourage young people to develop such love – by doing it ourselves – they respond beautifully. It is the kind of challenge that draws out their highest capacities.

Nevertheless, it does go against the grain of our human conditioning. We are conditioned to be always on guard, in case a certain somebody, a kind of thorn-in-the-flesh, might be coming around the next corner. If we see him we want to be ready to make our escape, duck out through the next door into a dark alley and disappear into the night.

Instead, when you have acquired this extraordinary skill, you are no longer ruled by fear. If you see Mr. Thorn approaching, you may actually decide to go and meet him. "He's going to be unpleasant," you say to yourself. "What an opportunity!" "She's going to be discourteous; I can help her by being courteous and calm."

When I used to present this in the early sixties, the beatniks of San Francisco, whom I liked very much, used to say, "Man, that's all topsy-turvy!"

"No," I used to say, "everything is topsy-turvy now. When you can act like this, then the world will be righted."

❦ A BRIDGE

*What wisdom can you find that is greater
than kindness?*

     – JEAN JACQUES ROUSSEAU

THROUGH CONSTANT PRACTICE IT IS
possible to make your life a permanent gift to your
family and the world. You can become a kind of
Christmas tree all year long. Any time your children or your partner or your parents are in pain
or discomfort, when they are afraid or uneasy,
they can come and help themselves to your love
and security.

It is not possible to achieve such inner peace
without becoming deeply aware of the needs of
those around you. Highly self-willed people always find it difficult to love because, while they
may have a bright intellect and a great deal of

wealth, they react immediately to the least provocation. If you are angry, they will retaliate. If you are afraid, they will be insecure. That's just human conditioning, which I sometimes call the jukebox response: you put in your quarter and the old, familiar tune comes out.

Some psychologists have claimed that stimulus and response is the basis of all human behavior. I disagree. There are some glorious exceptions – the great spiritual teachers of all the major religions, who have shown that if you want to love more and more, it is possible to cut the nexus between what others do to you and what you do to them.

According to these spiritual figures, in order to call yourself a lover, you must be free from the need to react; you must be free to respond as you consider best. If somebody is unkind to you, you can choose to be kind to that person, which is the best way to win him over. If somebody slanders you, you can choose not to be intimidated or up-set, but to bide your time and try to help her when she is calmer. That is what deep love can do.

You can see how much the world needs such people. Wherever they live, they will be a bridge between individuals, between races, even between nations. According to the English mystic William Law, such "love has no errors, for all errors are the want of love."

PART THREE

The Unity of Life

FROM WASTEFUL TO SIMPLE

HENRY DAVID THOREAU RAISED A PRO-
vocative question: "What is the use of a house if
you haven't got a tolerable planet to put it on?" It's
hard to answer. What is the use of science and art
and dancing and music if our way of life is making
the earth uninhabitable?

I love music and the fine arts; I have always been
a fan of classical dance and theater; I have deep
respect for the beneficial accomplishments of science. But all of these take second place in my heart
– not because I don't love the arts and sciences but
because, as Thoreau would say, if you don't have a
good planet to put it on, what's the use of having
the best home in California? Among all our activities our first priority should be to change our mode
of living from wasteful to simple, from thoughtless
to elegant, from destructive to sustainable.

It is not always glamorous work to slowly change your habits and help others to change theirs, to dismantle the old and quietly build a new life. Probably no one will give you a Nobel Prize or an Oscar for having worked to protect the earth, but deep inside you will feel the joy of having contributed. You will have won the respect of the hardest person to please in the world: yourself.

✿ SEEING THE UNITY OF LIFE

BEFORE I TOOK TO MEDITATION, I HAD read many times about the unity underlying the seeming diversity of life, both in Western and Eastern writers, but until I had travelled deep into my consciousness through meditation, I could not have believed that the world really is one, that all of us are one. The sun, the moon, the stars, the ocean, the rivers, the forests, we are all one family. That is the lesson our environmental crisis is trying to teach us.

Learning to see the unity of life is a little like breaking a secret code. When I was a boy scout in India, like boy scouts everywhere I had to learn Morse code. On a special occasion when the local school inspector came, my cousin and I were chosen to demonstrate our communications skills. The inspector gave me a message which I transmitted with flags to my cousin, who was standing fifty yards away. Dot dash dot, dot dot dash, and so forth. If an onlooker didn't know the code, he would have wondered why these fellows were waving their flags. But anyone who knew the code would be able to follow.

William Blake, who broke through life's code, said that when he looked at the rising sun he saw not just a glowing disk of fire somewhat like a guinea, but a host of angels singing, "Holy, Holy, Holy." If you tell William Blake that you don't hear the angels, he will say, "You have earplugs in your ears; how do you expect to hear? Pull them out and then you will hear."

Meditation enables us to interpret the code of all life. We learn to remove the earplugs and blindfold which keep us from knowing the unity. Gradually, we gain a new mode of perception.

When we look at a forest, for example, we begin to understand that botany is not the only way to study trees. Just as there is a biological aspect to trees, there is a spiritual aspect from which we can learn: it is a tree's nature to give. You and I give gifts on Christmas – only to people whom we like, and only when they have gifts for us. For a tree, however, it is Christmas every day and night. A fir tree doesn't say, "Here is oxygen only for people I like." A mango tree doesn't say, "I won't give you mangoes because you don't like me." They say to everybody, "Come help yourselves. What we give is free for all."

Gradually, we can learn to give something back to these trees to show them our love. That doesn't mean writing sonnets and hanging them on their trunks. To show love for trees means simply to speak their language: plant them, look after them, fertilize them, prune them, protect them, and let them grow to their full height. They will express their love by giving us oxygen and feeding us.

🌰 SEEING LOVE IN THE SUN

IN THE BHAGAVAD GITA THE LORD SAYS, "Among luminaries I am the sun." This is to remind us that we depend for our very life on the sun and the many physical and biological forces which filter and harness the sun's rays. In the traditional language of religion, this complex network of forces is beautiful proof of the Lord's love for us.

Without the sun, we would have no food. Everything we eat contains a generous helping of sunlight. The leaves of the plants and trees are solar collectors trained to catch the sun's energy and turn it into gourmet cuisine. Who but a lover would do all this? Just as on St. Valentine's Day you present your sweetheart with flowers, the Self, which lives in every one of those plants and trees, is giving us the very best food every day.

In the western tradition, St. Francis of Assisi gives beautiful expression to our kinship with the sun when he addresses it as Brother Sun. He is reminding us that all of us – even the stars and planets – belong to the same family. When we get carried away with personal profit and forget that we belong to this family, the results are always disastrous.

Whether you call it God's love, or Nature's providence, or lucky coincidence, the earth's stratospheric ozone layer is perfectly balanced to protect us against the sun's ultraviolet rays. Now, however, that protective shield is being severely damaged by industrial chemicals produced and used primarily to make a profit, and we have unwittingly disrupted the delicate network of forces which protect our health and future. Let us make sure this never happens again. There is a place for profit in every business, but our first concern should always be to keep our business and our lives in harmony with the forces which preserve life.

AT HOME IN THE UNIVERSE

Covet nothing. All belongs to the Lord.
Thus working may you live a hundred years.
Thus alone will you work in real freedom.

— ISHA UPANISHAD

IN SPIRITUAL TERMS, THE VERY TAPROOT of the environmental movement is that everything belongs to the one Self who lives in the hearts of all people and creatures, and even insects and plants.

In practical terms that means nothing on earth is ours to destroy. Nobody has any right to pollute the air, water, or seas, to cut down forests, or to wash away the topsoil. We do not own the earth. We are just transients who have been entrusted to leave the earth a little better than we found it. This is everybody's job; nobody is exempt from it and, in this sense, nobody is unemployed.

It follows that our environmental crisis demands that every one of us play a useful part, in our own way, to improve the environment wherever we live. If a person fails to do that, even if he makes a lot of money or if she wins a prestigious prize, the Buddha would say, "You haven't done what you have to do."

When you have done what you have to do, you will feel very secure, very fulfilled. As you discover the Self in your own heart, you discover it simultaneously everywhere, in the people and creatures around you. You will feel very much at home in this universe. You don't need to take my word for it. Try it and see for yourself.

YOUR ESSENCE IS KINDNESS

*Ahimsa (nonviolence) is for Gandhi the
basic law of our being. That is why it can be
used as the most effective principle for social
action, since it is in deep accord with the
truth of man's nature, and corresponds to
his innate desire for peace, justice, order,
freedom, and personal dignity.*

—THOMAS MERTON

WHEN I WAS TEACHING FRESHMEN IN MY
junior college in India, I noticed that they had a
curious difficulty: they would confuse the English
words "invent" and "discover." As I graded their
papers, I often ran across sentences like, "The
telescope was discovered by Galileo." I hit upon
a simple means of showing them the difference
between inventing and discovering.

I would take a piece of chalk in one hand, cover it, and say, "I have covered it. Now I open my hand, and you have discovered it." Afterwards they never said Galileo discovered telescopes.

The same is true for the abiding love –. what Gandhi called *ahimsa* – that dwells in the depths of our hearts. You don't have to invent it, or buy it, or borrow it, or steal it from a saint. You have already got it. It is in you, but it is covered so thickly that you don't suspect that your very nature is love, your very essence is kindness. This is the discovery that you make when you bring your mind to stillness through the practice of meditation and the allied disciplines.

Afterwards, you can function beautifully in all aspects of your life, living with your family, working at a clinic or a campus or a store, and be a living influence for kindness, goodness, and love, wherever you choose to play your part.

🍎 A LIFE OF PEACE

I have known from early youth that
nonviolence is not a cloistered virtue to
be practiced by the individual for his
peace and final salvation, but it is a rule
of conduct for the whole of society.

— MAHATMA GANDHI

USUALLY, THE CONCEPT OF NONVIOLENCE is applied only to violence between human beings or nations, but having experimented with it for many years, I have learned from Gandhi to apply it to almost all aspects of daily living.

The primary cause of the environmental crisis is our society's attitude that nature is ours to dominate and exploit for our own benefit. This is a great violence we do to the earth, a violence which needs to be opposed – gently but firmly

– with the nonviolence of a simple, sustainable life, lived in love and respect for all.

So what Gandhiji stands for when he places the ideal of ahimsa before us is not patchwork reform in politics or economics, changing a little here or there. Rather, he says, we must go deep within ourselves and change the very basis of our attitude towards the environment, towards others, towards ourselves.

"THEY AIN'T MAKIN' REAL ESTATE NO MORE"

THROUGH DEFORESTATION AND MODERN industrial agricultural methods – the methods of "agribusiness" – the world is losing billions of tons of topsoil every year. The United States is no exception. Every year we peel off another layer of skin from our Mother Earth. How long can it last? As an American humorist said, "They ain't makin' real estate no more."

I look back with great respect to the days of my boyhood in South India, when we were trained never to do anything to deprive our living Mother Earth of her skin. For us, agriculture was taught not only in schools and colleges. It was a way of life passed down from generation to generation, and every new generation had the opportunity to improve a little upon it. I have coined a phrase for this way of life: *agridharma*, from *agri*, meaning "field," and *dharma*, meaning "law or divine order." It is an entire way of life, which respects the needs of the earth and all creatures even as it seeks to fill the needs of human beings.

When you raise your own vegetables and fruits, when you buy locally grown organic produce, when you adopt a vegetarian diet to help protect the rain forests, you are helping to replace agri-business with agridharma, violence with love.

POSSESSED BY LOVE

Let me be possessed by love . . .

—THOMAS À KEMPIS

SPIRITUAL TEACHERS FROM ALL THE world's traditions are fond of warning us never to be possessed by things. If you look carefully at any paper or magazine you will see that, while our modern civilization has contributed a great deal towards making our life more comfortable, it has also been conditioning us slowly but surely not to possess things, but to be possessed by them. The conditioning can be easily observed. The proof is that when we think we cannot have something we want, whether it is a new dress or a new car, we feel inadequate, incomplete.

This strange inadequacy, which the media exploits, is the source of a popular modern phenomenon, impulse buying. You go to a shopping center to have a cup of cocoa, and you come back with a big brown bag full of things. If I ask you why, you answer, "They were on sale." I have never been able to understand the logic of this. If you don't need something, what does it matter whether it is on sale or whether you can have two for one or eight for seven? Such "bargains" appeal to that hidden feeling of inadequacy.

But we can free ourselves. As the mystics of all religions prove, when you begin to see the light of the Self – who lives not outside you but in the depths of your heart – shining on the mountains, the sea, the forests, and all living creatures, you will be free. Once this experience comes to you,

you will be free to love. Even when you need to buy things, you will remember not to be possessed by them, but to possess them in freedom.

♜ A GARBAGE EXPERIMENT

I WAS AMAZED TO READ THAT EVERY man, woman, and child in our country generates twice his or her weight in waste every day. This garbage habit affects not only our own country. Our growing refuse pile now spills over our borders through what is called "garbage imperialism." As our landfills fill up, we are sending our waste, much of it toxic, to poor countries desperate for the meager income it brings.

So I suggest that all of us perform a little experiment. Keep a waste journal. It's a very good project for children, and an even better project for adults, to observe and calculate how this mountain of waste is generated. Then gradually cut down your waste from two times your weight to one. You see, I am not a revolutionary but an evolutionary. Generate only enough waste to equal your weight. If you are more ambitious, you can reduce your weight.

This has nothing to do with capitalism or socialism or any other -ism; this has everything to do with love of children. Every child everywhere is entitled to the reasonable comforts of life. No child's country should be treated as a dump. I follow my grandmother's way of changing my habits: not being forced by laws or public opinion or peer pressure, but impelled by love.

■ CONTENTMENT

THE BUDDHA GIVES A COMPASSIONATE explanation for the impulse which keeps us buying and throwing away more and more things. He calls it "thirst" – a thirst that parches our souls. Madison Avenue encourages us to slake that thirst by drinking salt water.

Remember the words of Jesus to the woman at the well? When he was thirsty, the woman gave him cool water to drink. Jesus, by way of thanking her, says, "Whosoever drinketh of this water shall thirst again. But whosoever drinketh of the water that I shall give him shall never thirst." Once you become aware of the Self, your thirst is quenched. You no longer need anything from the world.

When I was walking with my wife around a big shopping center a few days ago, I told her that even if they offered me everything free, I really wouldn't want anything. That doesn't mean I don't like to buy things that are useful, comfortable, and necessary, or to make the best of my personal appearance, but I have no craving for those things.

Through many years of meditation, I now find my contentment within, and my thirst has been quenched. Instead of having a sense of inadequacy or incompleteness when faced with such a bewildering array of items, I feel a great joy wherever I look: How many beautiful jackets I don't need! How many pairs of shoes I don't even have to look at! I'm a free man. I can make original choices unpressured by the mass media.

I am not wealthy, but because of this precious skill, which anyone can learn, I know how it is to be a millionaire. Once I asked a millionaire friend of mine, "Tell me, what does it mean to be a millionaire?"

"Ah," she said, "I can tell you that: this feeling of

freedom, wherever I go." That's the kind of freedom I have, but it is not dependent on stocks or shares. It comes from within. My greatest desire is that everyone may discover the tremendous wealth that all of us possess within, simply by virtue of being a human being.

🐛 "HEART ROOTS" REVOLUTION

WHILE I ADMIRE SOME OF THE GREAT strides modern civilization has made, I must point out that our progress has involved a great deal of violence towards nature. When someone asks me to appraise modern life, I always place its conveniences and technical advances on one side of the balance and put the injury to nature on the other.

The prevailing opinion seems to be that technology is an end in itself. We use technology now on the slightest provocation, whether the situation truly warrants it or not: in medicine, education, cooking, entertainment, and sports.

By contrast, I take every opportunity to remind people that technology is only a means. It can never be an end. I am all for "high tech" when it is combined with high ideals, but it is up to people like you and me to say, very politely but persuasively, "If there is any suspicion that this product is detrimental to the environment, we won't buy it and we will ask our friends not to buy it." That is my way – no demonstrations or violence against anybody – just an appeal to people's good sense through love and education. That is the way a revolution can spread: not just growing from grass roots but from "heart roots" as well.

🐾 SLOW, SIMPLE, BEAUTIFUL, LOVING

THERE IS A CLOSE CONNECTION BETWEEN slowing down, living simply, and bringing beauty and love into our lives.

The economist E. F. Schumacher made a deep impression on millions of people with his book *Small Is Beautiful*, and I have often thought someone should write a companion volume called *Slow Is Beautiful*. As George Bernard Shaw used to ask, how is the person traveling three hundred miles per hour more civilized than the person traveling three miles per hour?

I am not a champion of poverty – no one anywhere should have to live in poverty – but I am a champion of simplicity. To me, the simple life is beautiful, artistic, and aesthetically satisfying. It produces the maximum effect with a minimum of means. Far too often our modern technology, despite its ingenuity, produces just the opposite: the minimum effect with the maximum of means. According to a saying in my mother tongue, Malayalam, we are using a sword to cut a ribbon.

This is not an issue for governments or corporations to solve. If every man and woman will try to simplify life in accordance with their needs and the context in which they live, they will find they have plenty of time to love.

Although "love" has become a common word today, it is frequently used without any understanding of what an uncommon thing it really is. People talk about falling in love like falling into a manhole. It's not at all that easy. We need time, a slow pace, and a simple life to gain some understanding of what love is.

⬛ TWO IN A CAR

BY NOW ALL OF US HAVE HEARD THE scientists' warnings that our industrial society releases so much carbon dioxide and other heat-trapping gases that our planet may become a kind of hothouse. This could have disastrous effects for all of life – if, that is, all of us don't join together to prevent it.

Governments and big business have an important role to play, but there is no need to wait for them. The answer is as close as the nearest freeway. Next time you go out for a ride, look around at the other cars. The vast majority carry only one person. To reduce your personal automotive emissions by fifty percent, all you need to do is follow a simple and elegant suggestion: don't drive alone – travel with at least two in a car.

That's where slowing down comes in. Carpooling often means that you have to go to your friend's home and wait a while – talk to the children, play with the dog. Perhaps it means starting a little earlier or going a little out of your way, but that is the art of living in wisdom. Waiting a few minutes for a friend gradually becomes a joy. You start thinking differently, not just about yourself and your time, but about your friends, the air, and the earth.

Of course there are some occasions when you will have to travel alone, but you can always be on the lookout for people to share your ride, your tires, your car, your company. I may be an unqualified idealist, but just imagine what a different scene there would be on the freeways if we could persuade people to travel four in a car! Day by day, little people like you and me can bring about a quiet, unobtrusive revolution.

🐦 GENTLENESS

*Blessed are the meek, for they shall inherit
the earth.*

— THE SERMON ON THE MOUNT

TO ME, THE WORD "MEEK" HERE MEANS
"gentle." Gentleness is a quality conspicuous by its
absence in our modern world. In order to be truly
gentle you have to be secure and in order to be
secure you have to be inwardly very strong.

When a great figure like Jesus speaks of gentleness, it is gentleness founded upon the rock of
strength. People who get angry easily, who threat-
en you and spread scandals about you, have no
toughness in them. Isn't Jesus called "Gentle Jesus,
meek and mild"? He can afford to be meek and
mild because his strength comes entirely from
within.

It's imperative for us to teach our children this because, for the most part, the media have given them models only of violence and anger, of people who either threaten or are intimidated. To quote T. S. Eliot, such people are all stuffed with straw. They have nothing inside. As your spiritual awareness grows, you will find you have a very gentle fellow-feeling for all creatures, because you will be growing in inner strength. More and more, you will find that you are protecting all those around you.

MOTHER EARTH

The human race is a family. Men are
brothers. All wars are civil wars.

— ADLAI STEVENSON

IN THE HINDU TRADITION, THE EARTH IS often referred to as a very patient woman. She has to bear with all our misdeeds. We are all her children. Perhaps there is no greater sorrow for a mother than to see her children quarreling among themselves. In my village, two brothers quarreling or two sisters quarreling will be taken up as a village issue, since this is considered to be something that should never happen; it's no longer a domestic issue, but a community one.

The word for sibling in many Indian languages means "together in the womb." They have lived in the same womb. So they should always help each other. Similarly, we all come from the womb of Mother Earth. We are all brothers and sisters.

Peace is not created by governments and fighting forces. Peace is made by little people like you and me getting to know other people, other countries, other races. Invite them into your homes, ask them about their country, and you'll find what I discovered after coming to the U.S. over thirty years ago.

When I went back to visit India my relatives and friends asked me, "How did you find people there?"

"Just as I find people here," I said.

"Really?"

"Yes. They like everybody to be kind to them; they like everybody to be good to them; they like peace among people; they like loving relationships among people."

This is what people in every country are looking

for. And after my talks in the early days in this country, friends would ask me the same question, "How do you like it here?" I replied, "The same as I liked it there. You and I have ninety-nine percent in common and a delightful one percent not in common."

All the wars and exploitation, the inability to communicate, and the competition for resources that now plague the world derive from that one percent of difference. Every day, by our words and actions, each of us can be a gentle reminder to the world of all that we have in common.

A HOUSE UNITED

SURELY THERE IS NO SPECTACLE MORE tragic than the one described by Abraham Lincoln as "a house divided against itself" – civil war. As

I write this book, dozens of countries are being torn asunder by it, with untold cruelties being inflicted upon men, women, and children. Many other countries are suffering from ethnic and racial tensions that flare into violence between neighbor and neighbor, family and family. Even the "first world" countries of America and Europe are not immune. In our highly armed, high-tech world, such conflicts pose a threat not just to our society, but to the earth and future generations.

As discouraging as they can be, we should remember that these are not clashes between armies but people, and that the most powerful way to transform people is not through violence or punishment or sanctions, but through patient personal example. Every one of us has a role to play in this great task, right in our own home and community. It doesn't require speaking or writing or political skills. It requires ideals and the desire to live by them. I can illustrate with an incident from my own life.

In the early days of my academic career, India was undergoing the agony of civil war between Muslims and Hindus. On the eve of the partition of Pakistan and India, I was posted to a college in central India not far from the University of Nagpur, where I had studied.

When I arrived on the campus, I went to the office and signed my contract. I knew nobody there, nor did I know the language, and I was wondering where on earth I would stay. I headed outside to a horse carriage, which was waiting with my luggage. I planned to return to town and look for a room in a hotel.

As I climbed into the carriage, I was surprised to see one of my dearest Muslim friends from college running towards me. Naimuddin and I had attended postgraduate school together and had lived in the same dorm. A gracious and modest man, he was a much better scholar than I, at home in Urdu, Persian, Arabic, and Turkish, but when I praised his linguistic and research skills, he would simply say, "I rob dead men's graves. You've got the living touch. Don't ever lose it."

So he jumped into my horse carriage and told the driver to go to his home. I was puzzled. "You're coming with me," he said, "and you're going to stay with me." That was all.

We arrived at his residence, a big medieval mansion entrusted to him by a *nawab,* a Muslim aristocrat, who had gone on pilgrimage to Mecca. I accepted his generous invitation and stayed.

But those were difficult, dangerous days for Hindus and Muslims. In some cities terrible violence had been unleashed, and on our campus the spirit of unity had received such a setback that Hindu and Muslim students used to sit on opposite sides of the classroom. Even the faculty was becoming polarized.

I should mention here that Naimuddin and I were not brave people. In fact, he was even less brave than I was, which is saying a good deal. But we had ideals, and we were prepared to stand by them. So we said, "Why shouldn't we stay together?" Many of my friends warned us, "You're both going to get hurt. Being idealistic is one thing, being practical is another." I disagreed then and I still disagree. Experience confirmed our faith in human nature. Not a single person caused us trouble.

Encouraged, Naimuddin and I undertook an experiment. In the evening, sitting together with a few other junior faculty members, Naimuddin would recite the *Rubaiyat of Omar Khayyam* in the beautiful Persian original. I would recite FitzGerald's excellent English translation. These great verses are irresistible to any poetry lover, and there were many poetry lovers in my classes, both Hindu and Muslim.

> Awake! for Morning in the Bowl of Night,
> Has flung the stone that puts the Stars
> to flight:
> And Lo! the Hunter of the East has caught
> The Sultan's Turret in a Noose of Light.

It was only a matter of time before the news spread. One by one, students began to wander by and stand in the door, then step in, then sit down. Eventually, a good crowd of Hindus and Muslims were gathered there every Saturday, sitting side by side, listening together to the verses.

During our tenure at that college – even when tensions were very high – Naimuddin and I per-severed. We shared the mansion. We walked to campus together. We recited poetry and staged plays together. And just because two people carried their ideals into practice, the atmosphere of the whole campus changed.

Years later I read about a terrible flood that swept away thousands of people in Kashmir, on both the Indian and Pakistani sides. I was deeply touched to read how Indian and Pakistani soldiers worked together to save lives and rescue cattle, forgetting past differences. In such events we glimpse the noblest part of human nature, our true personality. All the rest – the fighting, the retaliation, the vendettas – are nothing but a covering, a cloud of smoke obscuring our real Self.

It is my prayer that, through such cooperation, seemingly insignificant people like you and me will be able to dampen and eventually extinguish the fires of hatred which now trouble so many communities and countries. It doesn't take large numbers to change human relationships in any country, even today. It doesn't take government action to heal the earth. It takes dedication, determination, and a certain amount of faith in the goodness hidden in our hearts.

It takes you.

THE BLUE MOUNTAIN
CENTER OF MEDITATION

The Blue Mountain Center of Meditation publishes Easwaran's books, videos, and audios, and offers retreats on his eight-point program of passage meditation. For more information:

The Blue Mountain Center of Meditation

Box 256, Tomales, California 94971

Telephone: +1 707 878 2369

Toll-free in the US: 800 475 2369

Facsimile: +1 707 878 2375

Email: info@easwaran.org

www.easwaran.org

NILGIRI PRESS

TAKE YOUR TIME

Life today can feel so fragmented. Often we face enormous pressures both on the work front and at home. In *Take Your Time: How to Find Patience, Peace & Meaning*, Eknath Easwaran explains how, if we slow down, we can gain control over our minds and, gradually, over our lives as well.

Through his anecdotes and insights, he shows how to try something different the next time we feel stressed and speeded up.

Step back, slow down, and find a doorway to joy and serenity where you might never have thought to look.

NILGIRI PRESS

THE BOOKS OF EKNATH EASWARAN

GANDHI THE MAN

Easwaran, who grew up in Gandhi's India, tells the story of the Mahatma's self-transformation from a shy, ineffective lawyer into a fearless, wise leader – showing how we, too, can transform anger into compassion, hatred into love.

"Comes closer to giving some sense of how Gandhi saw his life than any other account I have read."

– BILL MCKIBBEN, *New York Post*

NILGIRI PRESS

THE BOOKS OF EKNATH EASWARAN

PASSAGE MEDITATION

"This is the secret of meditation: we become what we meditate on." — EKNATH EASWARAN

This is an introduction to Easwaran's method of passage meditation, in which we choose inspirational texts, or passages, that embody our highest ideals and send them deep into consciousness through slow, sustained attention. This method fits with any faith, philsophy, or lifestyle.

Carefully tested, practical and inspiring, *Passage Meditation* offers a complete program to help us stay calm, kind, and focused at work and at home.

NILGIRI PRESS

THE BOOKS OF EKNATH EASWARAN

WORDS TO LIVE BY

Start your day – or end it – with this warmly encouraging collection of inspirational quotations for each day, accompanied by Easwaran's commentaries.

These quotes come from some of history's most brilliant philosophers, poets, and sages from all traditions. Easwaran takes these timeless truths and illustrates them with contemporary examples, showing how we can apply these truths in our own lives to face our challenges with courage, compassion, and good judgment.

NILGIRI PRESS

THE BOOKS OF EKNATH EASWARAN

STRENGTH IN THE STORM

We can't always control what life sends us, but we can choose how we respond. And that, Easwaran tells us, is mainly a matter of quieting the agitation in the mind. It's a simple idea, but one that goes deep – a truly calm mind can weather any storm.

And we learn to calm the mind through practice – there's no magic about it. This book offers insights, stories, practical techniques, and exercises that will help us release the energy, compassion, and wisdom we need to ride the waves of life minute by minute, day by day.

NILGIRI PRESS

Eknath Easwaran (1910-1999) is respected around the world as an authentic teacher of timeless wisdom. His approach fits naturally into any faith, philosophy, or lifestyle.

Born in a small village in Kerala state, India, Easwaran grew up listening to his grandmother's age-old stories, and learned from her wise, loving example as she guided and supported her busy extended family. As a young man, Easwaran visited Gandhi in his ashram and was deeply influenced by the way he brought spiritual values into daily life.

Easwaran came to the United States on the Fulbright exchange program in 1959. In 1961 he founded the Blue Mountain Center of Meditation, which carries on his work today through publications and retreats. More than 1.4 million copies of his books are in print.

NILGIRI PRESS

Publisher's Cataloging-In-Publication Data

Easwaran, Eknath.

      Renewal : a little book of courage and hope / by Eknath Easwaran.
— 1st ed.

      p. ; cm. — (Pocket wisdom series)

      "The selections in this book are taken from Eknath Easwaran's Your
life is your message . . ."—t.p. verso
     I S B N: 978–1–58638–034–2

1. Meditations. 2. Conduct of life. 3. Ecology—Psychological aspects.
4. Transpersonal psychology. I. Easwaran, Eknath. Your life is your message.
II. Title.

BL624.2 .E38 2009
204.35   2008942445